Rain Forests Around the World

Mary Kate Bolinder

Consultants

Doris Namala, Ph.D.
Assistant Professor of History
Riverside City College

Olivia Tolich
Subject Matter Expert, K–6
Pearson Australia

Brian Allman
Principal
Upshur County Schools, West Virginia

Publishing Credits

Rachelle Cracchiolo, M.S.Ed., *Publisher*
Emily R. Smith, M.A.Ed., *SVP of Content Development*
Véronique Bos, *Vice President of Creative*
Dani Neiley, *Editor*
Fabiola Sepulveda, *Series Graphic Designer*

Image Credits: p.6 Alamy/Ivan Sebbornl; p.8 (bottom) Alamy/Pedro Helder; p.10 Alamy/
Worldwide Picture Library; p.11 (top) Getty Images/Avalon; p.11 (bottom) Alamy/Hemis;
p.12 (top) Alamy/Universal Images Group North America LLC/DeAgostini; p.12 (bottom)
Alamy/Pulsar Imagens; p.13 Getty Images/Joao Laet; p.14 Joel Rogers (joelrogers.com);
p.15 (top) Alamy/Friedrich von Hörsten; p.15 (bottom) Getty Images/Cris Bouroncle;
pp.16–17 Alamy/Ian Dagnall; p.19 Alamy/Morley Read; p.20 (top) Alamy/BrazilPhotos;
p.23 Anadolu Agency; p.25 (left) Alamy/Mark Phillips; p.25 (right) Alamy/Jeremy Sutton-
Hibbert; all other images from iStock and/or Shutterstock

Library of Congress Cataloging-in-Publication Data

Names: Bolinder, Mary Kate, author.
Title: Rain forests around the world / Mary Kate Bolinder.
Description: Huntington Beach, CA : Teacher Created Materials, [2023] |
  Includes index. | Audience: Ages 8-18 | Summary: "Explore rain forests
  around the world! Travel to the Amazon, the world's largest rain forest.
  Discover the natural wonders found there. Did you know that over half
  the world's plant and animal species live in rain forests? Find out more
  about rain forests, and learn how how to protect and preserve these
  natural lands"-- Provided by publisher.
Identifiers: LCCN 2022038420 (print) | LCCN 2022038421 (ebook) | ISBN
  9781087695204 (paperback) | ISBN 9781087695365 (ebook)
Subjects: LCSH: Rain forests--Juvenile literature. | Rain forest
  ecology--Juvenile literature.
Classification: LCC QH541.5.R27 B65 2023 (print) | LCC QH541.5.R27
  (ebook) | DDC 577.34--dc23/eng/20221011
LC record available at https://lccn.loc.gov/2022038420
LC ebook record available at https://lccn.loc.gov/2022038421

**Shown on the cover is a rain forest
in Malaysia.**

5482 Argosy Avenue
Huntington Beach, CA 92649
www.tcmpub.com
ISBN 978-1-0876-9520-4
© 2023 Teacher Created Materials, Inc.

Table of Contents

Hoh Rain Forest, Olympic National Park, Washington

Welcome to the Rain Forest

The air is hot and sticky. Monkeys screech in the trees. Birds squawk high above you. The hum of insect wings is a constant sound. Thunder rolls in the distance as rain trickles down on you. All these things and more are part of daily life in tropical rain forests.

Hoh Rain Forest

tropical rain forest

temperate rain forest

Amazon Rain Forest

Congo River Basin Rain Forest

Rain forests have existed on Earth for over 100 million years. Rain forests can be found on six of the world's continents. They are the oldest **ecosystems** on the planet. They are diverse and delicate areas of land. More than half the world's plant and animal species live in rain forests. Trees in rain forests provide oxygen and help regulate Earth's **climate**.

Learning more about how rain forests grow and change is important. Human actions have affected the health of rain forests. Modern technology and population demands pose a threat to life in rain forests today. People, animals, and the planet need rain forests to survive.

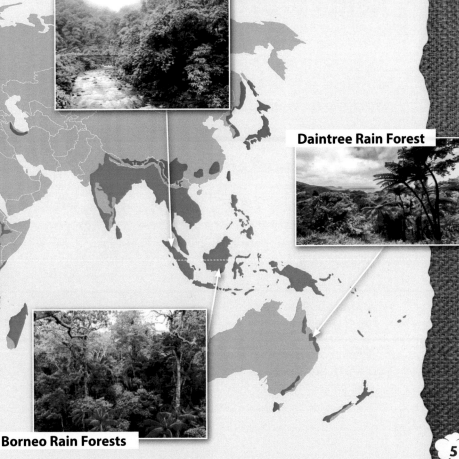

Sumatran Rain Forests

Daintree Rain Forest

Borneo Rain Forests

Catarata del Toro
waterfall in Costa Rica

Rain Forest Climates

What do you think the climate is like in tropical rain forests? If you guessed hot and humid, you are right! As their name suggests, rain forests get *a lot* of rain. Rain forests can be found in places where average yearly rainfall exceeds 70 to 100 inches (178 to 254 centimeters). Some seasons get more rain than others.

The Amazon Rain Forest

The Amazon Rain Forest is the largest rain forest in the world. It is located on the continent of South America near the equator. The Amazon Rain Forest is a tropical rain forest. The **tropics** are areas on Earth just north and south of the equator.

Amazon Rain Forest

In the Amazon, most of the rain falls between October and May. Rain falls over 200 days a year there. Sometimes, it rains for just a few minutes. Other storms can last for hours.

Rain is essential to life in the Amazon. Millions of trees, plants, and animals depend on the water to survive. Most of the trees and plants in the Amazon are **evergreen**. Evergreen trees do not lose their leaves. They continue to grow all year. They depend on a steady supply of water to grow. People and animals in the Amazon depend on water, too. Without the right amount of rainfall, life in the Amazon Rain Forest would not thrive.

Temperate Rain Forests

Tropical rain forests are not the only type of rain forest. **Temperate** rain forests also exist. They are much colder and less rainy than rain forests in tropical climates. Temperate rain forests are not as dense as tropical rain forests.

Plant and Animal Life

Rain forests can be divided into four layers. The highest layer is the emergent layer. The tops of the tallest trees can be found there. The trees can sometimes grow to more than 200 feet (60 meters) tall, but this is rare. Most of the treetops are found in the next layer, which is the canopy. The third layer is the understory. It is darker there because most of the sunlight is blocked by the trees above. It can also be wet in the understory from rain trickling down through the trees. Rain also drips down to the forest floor, which is the last layer. Both the understory and the forest floor are damp and humid.

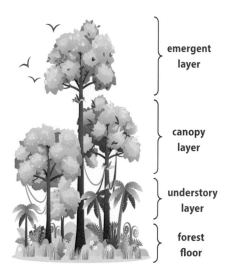

emergent layer

canopy layer

understory layer

forest floor

In the Amazon, most of the animals live in the canopy. Here, you will find colorful toucans, slow sloths, and loud howler monkeys. They eat the many fruits and leaves in the canopy. Butterflies and other insects, such as beetles, feed on flower nectar. Land animals, such as jaguars and tapirs, live along the forest floor.

jaguar in the Amazon

gorillas in the Congo Basin

The second-largest rain forest in the world is in the Congo Basin. This is in central Africa. Animals such as gorillas, chimpanzees, and elephants call this rain forest home. Their habitats are found in the bottom two rain forest layers.

There are also large rain forests on the islands of Borneo and Sumatra in Asia. Orangutans are found there. They spend most of their time in the trees of the understory layer. To stay safe from predators, they use vines and branches to swing between trees.

Big Bugs!

The Amazon Rain Forest is home to many unique insects. The Hercules beetle is one of them. It is one of the largest insects in the world. It can grow up to 7 inches (17.8 centimeters) long. This beetle is very strong. It can lift up to 850 times its own body weight! It eats rotting fruit and wood found on the ground.

Indigenous Peoples of the Amazon

Indigenous peoples have lived in the Amazon for thousands of years. They live in small **tribes** throughout the forest. The rain forest provides them with everything they need to survive. They make shelter from leaves and trees. Clothing is made from plant fiber. They find food among the many fruits and plants of the forest. Small animals and fish are also hunted for food. Plants provide medicine for illnesses. Estimates vary, but it is thought that more than one million Indigenous peoples live in the Amazon today.

The Kayapó

The Kayapó have lived in harmony with the land for generations. They use a method of controlled burning to create fertile farmland. The men of the tribe cut down and burn the trees in a small area. The ashes fertilize the ground. The women of the tribe plant fast-growing crops in the rich soil. With careful planting, weeding, and burning, the same land can be farmed for several years. Over time, the soil may lose nutrients. This makes it harder to plant the same crops. If that happens, different crops can be planted. Or the land can be left alone so the forest plants can begin to regrow.

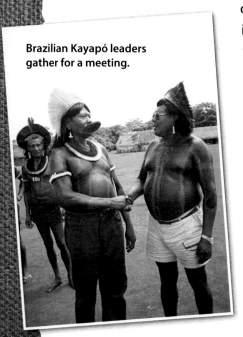
Brazilian Kayapó leaders gather for a meeting.

The Kayapó also use modern-day items, such as motorboats, fishing equipment, and cooking tools. Many of them wear modern clothes along with traditional body paint.

In the Amazon, land is carefully cleared and burned to create space for homes and agriculture.

Some Indigenous peoples have refused attempts to connect with the outside world.

Uncontacted Tribes

There are still many uncontacted tribes living in the Amazon. This means they have not come into contact with western civilization. Or they have rejected attempts to meet. The majority of these tribes live near the border between Peru and Brazil.

Two Yanomami men travel by canoe in the Amazon River basin.

The Yanomami

The Yanomami are an Indigenous tribe. They live in Brazil and Venezuela. Their civilization is similar to the Kayapó. One crop they grow is tobacco. They live in **thatched** houses. But, their houses are not permanent homes. When the soil around their houses wears out, the Yanomami move their villages to new spots.

In the 1980s, gold miners invaded Yanomami territory. The Yanomami fought to protect their land. Many people died. Others died from new diseases brought by the miners. The Yanomami still fight to keep miners off their land.

a Yanomami thatched house

Kayapó men protest in Brazil to end illegal mining and deforestation.

Native Lands

The tribes of the Amazon want to protect their land. The government has granted protection to parts of the rain forest. However, **deforestation** hit a 15-year high in 2021. More and more of the Amazon is destroyed every day. Many big companies do not always follow the rules that protect the forest. People cut down trees. Miners build roads and mine without permission. Groups, such as the Amazon Conservation Team, help Indigenous peoples protect their land. They encourage the government and other agencies to change their destructive ways. They hope the land will be protected from deforestation. Protecting the Amazon helps the tribes keep their ways of life.

Protecting Native Lands

In 2019, the Waorani people of Ecuador sued their country's government. The government was trying to sell their land to a big oil company. The Waorani won the case. Now, their land and way of life are protected.

Life in Rain Forests of the World

Indigenous peoples also live in other rain forests around the world. Scientists and tourists are part of life in these forests as well. Many people work in and visit these rain forests.

Life in the Hoh Rain Forest

The Hoh Rain Forest is on the Olympic Peninsula in Washington State. It is a temperate rain forest. Ferns cover the ground, and moss grows on trees. Coniferous and **deciduous** trees grow there.

The Hoh Rain Forest was part of a rain forest chain. The chain once ran from southeastern Alaska to the central coast of California. Now, the Hoh Rain Forest is almost all that remains of this forest chain.

The Hoh Tribe is a group of native peoples who have lived in the area for thousands of years. Today, members of the Hoh Tribe make a living by fishing, crabbing, and clamming. They are also skilled basket makers and wood carvers.

The Hoh Tribe participates in the Tribal Canoe Journey in Olympia, Washington.

Mbuti Pygmies in the Congo Basin

Life in the Congo Basin

The Ituri Rain Forest is at the northeastern part of the Congo Basin. A group of Indigenous Pygmy peoples called the Mbuti have lived there for nearly 4,500 years. They are a nomadic tribe. The Mbuti make their homes by forming long sticks into rounded shapes. They cover these domes with large leaves.

The Mbuti are hunter-gatherers. They coexist with traditional farmers. The Mbuti trade forest resources with **agriculturalists**. They trade in exchange for items they need. These include crops, clothing, and tools. Some Mbuti choose to leave the rain forest. They may become farmers or live in permanent villages.

Time for School

There are not always roads that go through and into rain forests. So, some children who live near rain forests around the world get to school in unique ways. A small  group of children in Colombia take a zipline across the rain forest canopy. A few students in Indonesia walk across a rope line. Some students in the Philippines take a boat to school.

Male cassowaries incubate their eggs and care for the chicks.

Rain Forest Tourism

People from around the world visit rain forests each year. People want to learn how they can help **conserve** wildlife and plants in rain forests. This type of travel is called **ecotourism**.

Tourists like to visit the Daintree Rain Forest in Australia. At 180 million years old, it is the oldest rain forest on Earth. People come to observe the plants and animals that live there. Some species, such as the Green Dinosaur fruit tree, have been on Earth for more than 120 million years. This species existed when dinosaurs roamed the planet!

Ecotourism guides in the Daintree Rain Forest teach people about the ways of the Kuku Yalanji. They are the Indigenous peoples who live in the rain forest. The guides share how these people use the plants, fruits, and animals for survival.

Up, Up, and Away!

Scientists go to great lengths to protect the land they study. They need to observe the canopy of a rain forest, but they do not want to disturb the animals and plants. So, they use different methods to access the canopy. Hot air balloons can be used to give scientists a bird's-eye view of the area. In certain places, towers and walkways have been built. Scientists may use ropes and harnesses to move around safely.

Rain Forest Scientists

Scientists work in rain forests around the world. In some of them, they have created **biosphere** reserves. Think of a biosphere as a round target. In the center is an area that is protected from change. Scientists keep a close watch on this core area. The next ring is called a buffer zone. In this zone, tribes can live. Scientists can study the land and people. Scientists can receive training and learn from their research. Tourists can visit this zone as long as they do not interrupt observations. The next zone is called a transition zone. This is where towns, farms, and roads can be found. By doing research throughout each zone, scientists can work together to find **sustainable** solutions for life and work near rain forests.

core area

buffer zone

transition zone

Biosphere Reserve

research   education and training   tourism   human settlement

Resources from Rain Forests

Rain forests have many resources that people need. Around 20 percent of the world's fresh water flows through the Amazon River. This water also flows through its **tributaries**. Rain forests provide shelter, food, and safety. This is true for both people and animals. People use thousands of resources from rain forests in many ways.

cacao pods

Hass avocado tree

palm fruit and palm oil

Where Does Fruit Come From?

The next time you are at a grocery store, take a look in the produce section. Find a tropical fruit, and look for a sticker. Usually, the sticker will tell you where the fruit was grown. What country did it come from? Is it from a country that has rain forests?

tropical fruit stand

Fruits and Plants

On cleared rain forest land, certain fruits can be grown. These fruits are enjoyed around the world. Bananas, avocados, and mangoes all grow in rain forests. Coffee, cocoa, and vanilla come from rain forests, too. Doctors and scientists rely on some plants from rain forests for medicine. Millions of different plant species have been identified in rain forests. There are still many more to discover!

Nonrenewable Resources

The Amazon is filled with **nonrenewable resources**. Once these resources are gone, they cannot be replaced. Some minerals found in the Amazon are nonrenewable. Iron ore and copper are buried deep in the ground. Iron is used to make steel. Copper is used for electronics. There are also precious metals, such as gold. Gold is used for jewelry, money, and artwork.

gold mining machine in Ecuador

Mines have been built in rain forests to find these minerals and metals. But there can be negative effects. Sometimes, mining pollutes nearby waterways.

Farming in Rain Forests

Modern demands for food have increased the amount of farms in rain forests. In the Amazon, trees are cut down to make space for cattle farming and ranching. Cattle need large areas of cleared land to graze. Soy **plantations** also take up much of the cut forest. Soy is grown to feed **domesticated** animals. In fact, animals eat more soy than people do! People grow other crops in rain forests. There are coffee and sugar plantations in rain forests in South America, Africa, and Indonesia.

soy plantation in Brazil

cattle ranch in Brazil

hydroelectric dam on the
Pastaza River in Ecuador

Rain Forests and Energy

The Amazon River is one of the longest rivers in the world.
Many **dams** have been built on smaller rivers connected to
it. Power from the rushing water is turned into hydroelectric
energy. This energy powers much of Brazil. This type of energy
is renewable. However, it has some downsides. If dams are
not used well, they can cause flooding. This endangers nearby
animals and people. Dams can also cause smaller rivers to dry up.

Trees are another rain forest resource that is used for energy.
They can be turned into firewood or charcoal. People around
the world use these materials for heating and other energy
needs.

Wow, Cow!

Cows eat about 20 pounds
(9 kilograms) of food a day.
Cattle farmers must have
an enormous food supply to
keep all their cows healthy
and fed.

Preserving Rain Forests

Each year, thousands of trees are cut down in rain forests. It is estimated that nearly 60 percent of trees in the Amazon will be cut down by 2030. The reason for these trees being cut down is that the world's population is growing. More people means a greater need for food and water. Humans need shelter and fuel. As these demands for space increase, more trees are lost.

Deforestation

Deforestation is the process of removing trees to use the land for a new purpose. Rain forest trees can be cut down for many reasons. Trees are cut down to make room for cattle ranches and palm oil plantations. Trees are removed for lumber. Clearing trees can make space for people to build mines, dams, and roads. Sometimes, fires can cause the loss of trees. Deforestation has many negative effects on rain forests and the world. It can cause drought and stop the growth of plants. It may cause soil **erosion**. This can lead to flooding. With fewer trees, animals that live in the area have less food and shelter. Many animals, such as orangutans, are endangered because deforestation slowly takes their habitats away.

There is a delicate balance between protecting and using natural resources in rain forests. Trees are a renewable resource. They can be planted again. But taking too many of them away harms the land. It harms the people and animals who live there, too.

illegal deforestation in the Amazon

orangutans in
Sumatra, Indonesia

Disappearing Habitats

Tigers, rhinoceroses, elephants, and orangutans live in the
rain forests of Indonesia. Their habitats are being quickly
destroyed. Rain forests are being cut down to make palm oil
plantations. It is estimated that less than half of the rain forests
in Indonesia remain. Close to 2.5 million acres (1.1 hectares)
of land are lost each year.

Conservation

Conservationists are people who work to protect natural resources. Rain forest conservationists are always looking for new ways to protect rain forests. They look at the relationships between humans and rain forests. They want to make them more sustainable. One way they help is by planting new trees. But this process is slow. It can take many years for the trees to be as tall and healthy as they once were. Organizations around the world work to plant new trees in rain forests. They hope to help restore these forests.

Conservationists help in other ways, too. They can help create protected areas. These areas are protected by law from deforestation. Conservationists also help animals. Some species are endangered. They are at risk of becoming extinct. So, conservationists carefully watch over them. They help protect their habitats. They watch the species until the population increases.

poison dart frog

Animals in Danger

There are more than 2,000 endangered animals in the Amazon. Some endangered animals include jaguars, macaws, and poison dart frogs. Scientists are working to protect their habitats. They want to prevent the animals from becoming extinct.

How Can You Help?

People around the world can help protect rain forests. They can help by using fewer resources found in rain forests. This includes eating less meat. People can also avoid using palm and soybean oils. Using fewer paper products helps, too. Researching companies before buying goods from them is a helpful strategy. Some companies create goods in more sustainable ways than others. These companies may be more environmentally friendly. They may use less paper or cardboard in their packaging. Also, some companies donate part of their profits to support rain forests.

There are also many conservation groups to support. People can donate money to these groups. Some people volunteer their time to support them. People can also show their support on social media.

People around the world protest in support of rain forests.

25

Earth Needs Rain Forests

The rain forests of the world have grown and changed over thousands of years. The greatest danger to rain forests has occurred in the last century. Rapid deforestation is a major threat. It has caused rain forests to shrink in size over the years. But they are still home to diverse groups of people, animals, and plants. People living in and near rain forests around the world depend on the health of the forests to maintain their ways of life. More species of plants and animals are found in rain forests than anywhere else on Earth. And in some rain forests, new discoveries are made every year. Scientists completed a study in the Amazon between 2014 and 2015. They found a new plant or animal species every two days!

The natural resources from rain forests are used around the world. Conservationists work together to protect the fragile plants and animals found there. Protecting and preserving rain forests helps take care of *all* life on Earth. And rain forests help maintain a healthy climate for Earth, too.

Making small changes today, as well as pushing for large-scale change, can help save rain forests for future generations.

This rain forest in Malaysia is being destroyed to create room for palm oil plantations.

Young Conservationists

Students all over the world are working to protect rain forests. Students can write letters to government leaders and big companies to encourage change. Simple acts, such as reducing, reusing, and recycling, can have a big impact on the climate and the world.

Map It!

Rain forests provide many natural resources that humans need to survive and thrive. Look back through the book to review the many resources that come from rain forests around the world. With a partner, choose a continent and a rain forest. Then, make a resource map.

1. Choose a continent: Africa, Asia, Australia, Europe, North America, or South America. Then, choose a rain forest you will map.

2. Draw or trace a map of the rain forest on a sheet of paper. Make sure you include all the countries the rain forest is in.

3. Lightly shade and label the rain forest on the map.

4. Draw small graphics to represent important places and resources that can be found in the rain forest. For example, you might draw a banana if bananas grow in the rain forest you've chosen.

5. Create a map key with the graphics you've drawn, and label them.

6. Share your resource map with the class.

7. **Bonus:** Answer the following questions with your partner on the back of your map: Which resources are the most important to conserve? Which resources can people try to use less of, and why?

Daintree National Park

Australia

KEY

 Daintree National Park

 bananas

 Daintree Discovery Centre

Glossary

agriculturalists—people who produce crops and raise livestock

biosphere—a part of Earth where life exists

climate—the weather patterns of a place or region

conserve—to save or use less

dams—large walls or barriers that hold back water

deciduous—trees that shed and regrow leaves every year

deforestation—the action of clearing or removing all trees from an area

domesticated—tamed and kept on a farm or as a pet

ecosystems—groups of living and nonliving things that make up environments and affect each other

ecotourism—a form of tourism that is mindful of protecting natural environments

erosion—the process of wearing away land by natural forces, such as ice or water

evergreen—having leaves that remain green through more than one growing season

Indigenous—from or native to a particular area

nonrenewable resources—natural resources that cannot be replaced

plantations—large areas where people work to grow crops

sustainable—able to be maintained without damaging the environment

temperate—relating to an area or climate with mild temperatures

thatched—covered in natural fibers, such as straw

tribes—groups of Indigenous peoples that include many families and relatives who have the same language, customs, and beliefs

tributaries—rivers that flow into a larger river

tropics—parts of the world near the equator where the weather is very warm

ruins of Tikal in Guatemala's tropical rain forest

Index

Learn More!

Marina Silva is an activist and politican who grew up in the Amazon Rain Forest. At age 16, Silva learned to read and write. She was the first person in her family to do so. She led peaceful protests against deforestation. She spoke out to protect the lands of Indigenous communities. She was the youngest person elected to Brazil's Senate. During her career, Silva has worked to protect rain forests. She also works to protect the people who live there.

- Research Silva's life and the events that led her to become an activist for environmental change.

- Make a time line to show important events in Silva's life.

- Include at least 10 events on your time line. Start at Silva's childhood and end in the present day.

mangrove trees in the Amazon